Mr. Lincoln:
The Life of Abraham Lincoln

Allen C. Guelzo, Ph.D.

THE
GREAT
COURSES®

PUBLISHED BY:

THE GREAT COURSES
Corporate Headquarters
4840 Westfields Boulevard, Suite 500
Chantilly, Virginia 20151-2299
Phone: 1-800-832-2412
Fax: 703-378-3819
www.thegreatcourses.com

Allen C. Guelzo, Ph.D.

Henry R. Luce Professor of the Civil War Era
and Director of Civil War Era Studies, Gettysburg College

Dr. Allen C. Guelzo is the Henry R. Luce Professor of the Civil War Era and Director of Civil War Era Studies at Gettysburg College in Gettysburg, Pennsylvania. He is also the Associate Director of the Civil War Institute at Gettysburg College. He was born in Yokohama, Japan, but grew up in Philadelphia. He holds an M.A. and Ph.D. in history from the University of Pennsylvania, where he wrote his dissertation under the direction of Bruce Kuklick, Alan C. Kors, and Richard S. Dunn. Dr. Guelzo has taught at Drexel University and, for 13 years, at Eastern University in St. Davids, Pennsylvania. At Eastern, he was the Grace Ferguson Kea Professor of American History, and from 1998 to 2004, he was the founding dean of the Templeton Honors College at Eastern.

Dr. Guelzo is the author of numerous books on American intellectual history and on Abraham Lincoln and the Civil War era, beginning with his first work, *Edwards on the Will: A Century of American Theological Debate, 1750–1850* (Wesleyan University Press, 1989). His second book, *For the Union of Evangelical Christendom: The Irony of the Reformed Episcopalians, 1873–1930* (Penn State University Press, 1994), won the Outler Prize for Ecumenical Church History of the American Society of Church History. He wrote *The Crisis of the American Republic: A History of the Civil War and Reconstruction* for the St. Martin's Press American History series in 1995 and followed that with an edition of Josiah G. Holland's *Life of Abraham Lincoln* (1866) in 1998 for the "Bison Books" series of classic Lincoln biography reprints of the University of Nebraska Press. Dr. Guelzo's book *Abraham Lincoln: Redeemer President* (Wm. Eerdmans, 1999) won both the Lincoln Prize and the Abraham Lincoln Institute Prize in 2000. In 2003, his article, "Defending Emancipation: Abraham Lincoln and the Conkling Letter, August, 1863," won *Civil War History*'s John T. Hubbell Prize for the best article of that year. His most recent work, *Lincoln's Emancipation Proclamation: The End of Slavery in America* (Simon & Schuster, 2004), also won the Lincoln Institute Prize and the Lincoln Prize for 2005, making him the first double Lincoln Laureate in the history of both prizes. He is now at work on a new book on the Lincoln-Douglas debates of 1858, also for Simon & Schuster.

Dr. Guelzo has written for *The Washington Post*, the *Los Angeles Times*, *The Wall Street Journal*, *First Things*, the *Claremont Review of Books*, and *Books and Culture* and has been featured on NPR's "Weekend Edition Sunday" and Brian Lamb's "Booknotes." He is a member of the Board of Directors of the Abraham Lincoln Association, the Abraham Lincoln Institute, and the Historical Society of the Episcopal Church; a member of the advisory councils of the Abraham Lincoln Bicentennial Commission and the McNeil Center for Early American Studies (at the University of Pennsylvania); and a member of the American Historical Association, the Organization of American Historians, the Society for Historians of the Early American Republic, the Society of Civil War Historians, and the Union League of Philadelphia. Dr. Guelzo has been a fellow of the American Council of Learned Societies (1991–1992), the McNeil Center for Early American Studies (1992–1993), the Charles Warren Center for American Studies at Harvard University (1994–1995), and the James Madison Program in American Ideals and Institutions at Princeton University (2002–2003). Together with Patrick Allitt and Gary W. Gallagher, Dr. Guelzo team-taught The Teaching Company's new edition of its American History series, and he is completing a series in 2005 for The Teaching Company, *The American Mind*, on American intellectual history.

Dr. Guelzo lives in Paoli and Gettysburg, Pennsylvania, with his wife, Debra.

Table of Contents
Mr. Lincoln: The Life of Abraham Lincoln

Mr. Lincoln: The Life of Abraham Lincoln

Scope:

This Teaching Company lecture series offers an introduction to Abraham Lincoln, the 16th president of the United States and one of the most representative men our nation has produced. The 12 lectures of this course concentrate on opening up a view into the thinking and career of Lincoln, and they are built around four important themes:

1. What was it like to know Abraham Lincoln?

2. What ideas were at the core of his understanding of American politics?

3. Why did he oppose slavery, and what propelled him, in the 1850s, into the open opposition to slavery that led to his election to the presidency in 1860?

4. What particular gifts equipped Lincoln to lead the nation through the "fiery trial" of the Civil War?

This series falls into three parts: Lectures One through Four cover Lincoln's youth and maturation into a successful and self-made lawyer in Illinois, a man who was marked by a complex inner life and a tremendous thirst for accomplishment in politics. The second section (Lectures Five through Seven) focuses on Lincoln in the crucial decade of the 1850s, when he awakes to the threat posed to the future of the United States by slavery and rapidly advances to the front of the national stage. The last section covers Lincoln's presidency, his triumphant management of both emancipation and the restoration of the Union, and his legacy to modern times.

We will begin in Lecture One by looking into Lincoln's early years for the origins of some of his most noticeable traits: his love for words; his uneasy relationship with his father, Thomas, and his rejection of his father's religion and politics; his determination to reach for self-improvement through participation in the American "market revolution"; and the ease with which he attracted friends and allies in his quest for self-improvement. Lecture Two extends our acquaintance with Lincoln into his 20s and his first plunge into Illinois politics. We will pay particular attention to Henry Clay's Whig Party and why Lincoln pledged himself to Clay's revolutionary political and economic agenda. Lincoln's decision, at virtually the same time, to begin studying and practicing law is the hinge on which we will turn to Lecture Three. There, we will see what a peculiar mixture of success and failure accompanied Lincoln's life in the 1840s and 1850s—a strategic political marriage that yielded him deep private grief, election to Congress followed by political failure, and a highly lucrative law practice that did little to assuage the sorrow he felt for the deaths of his father and son. Finally, in Lecture Four, we will look closely at aspects of Lincoln's personality: his mixture of public ambition and private reticence, his obsession with logic and honesty, and his belief in *fatalism* and *scientific materialism* but his distaste for the fact that slavery denied opportunities for self-betterment.

We begin a new section in Lecture Five, in which the issue of American slavery rapidly comes to dominate Lincoln's horizons. This lecture explains how slavery, which the Founders expected would die out on its own, found a second wind in the 19th century through the amazing popularity of cotton as an international commodity. Riding this new wave of profitability, the slave states of the Union demanded increased space for legalized slavery, first in agitating for a war against Mexico (and the acquisition of Mexico's northern provinces as future slave states) and, second, by jettisoning the antislavery prohibitions of the Compromise of 1820 and permitting slavery to expand into the Louisiana Purchase territories of Kansas and Nebraska. Lincoln denounced the Kansas-Nebraska Act of 1854 as a betrayal of the intentions of the Founders and the perpetuation of a great moral injustice. As we see in Lecture Six, however, Lincoln found little or no support from the collapsing Whig Party. Convinced that a *Slave Power* was attempting to hijack the federal government, Lincoln joined the new antislavery Republican Party in 1856. Two years later, he was nominated to run for the U.S. Senate against the architect of the Kansas-Nebraska Act, Stephen A. Douglas. Though Douglas eked out a technical victory over Lincoln, the seven debates Lincoln and Douglas held through the campaign brought Lincoln national attention. Lecture Seven begins with Lincoln rising from the defeat of 1858 to become a dark-horse candidate for the Republican presidential nomination in 1860, and thanks to the self-inflicted divisions of the Democratic Party, Lincoln was able to win the presidential election with little more than a third of the votes cast but with a sizeable majority in the Electoral College.

Lecture Eight brings us to the last portion of the series, beginning with Lincoln's unhappy realization that the country he has just been elected to preside over is quickly tearing apart. Lincoln struggled to stave off the secession of the slave states, then tried to keep secession from becoming an armed confrontation. When the slave states' new Confederacy finally launched an attack on Fort Sumter, Lincoln called out the army, the state militias, and state volunteers. And though the first federal military moves ended in defeat at Bull Run, Lincoln found a general—George B. McClellan—whom he believed had the competence to win the war. Lecture Nine shows just how mistaken Lincoln was in McClellan, who was unwilling to take military risks and even more unwilling to endorse political risks, especially any move by Lincoln to link the emancipation of the Confederacy's slaves to the war. Lincoln had begun tinkering with emancipation schemes early in his presidency, but McClellan's failures compelled Lincoln to accelerate his plans for emancipation, and he issued an Emancipation Proclamation on January 1, 1863, shortly after sacking McClellan.

McClellan, as we see in Lecture Ten, was only one of Lincoln's problems in winning the war. But Lincoln was able to draw on reservoirs of personal strength to renew his resolve for the task, and in Lecture Eleven, we look particularly at his greatest asset, his enormously persuasive way with words. This skill, however, could not guarantee Lincoln automatic success. He turned to General Ulysses Grant to command the federal armies in 1864, but Grant bogged down almost as ineffectively as McClellan, and Lincoln became convinced by the summer of 1864 that he was likely to lose a campaign for reelection. In the early fall, however, the fortunes of war changed dramatically. A string of military victories turned voters back to Lincoln, and in Lecture Twelve, we see Lincoln and Grant pushing the war to a successful conclusion in the spring of 1865. Lincoln's moment of triumph was brief; he was assassinated by a Confederate sympathizer and buried amid scenes of national mourning. But Lincoln had created a national legacy, and we close the series by reflecting on the enduring value of his affirmations of an open, democratic society of equals who are wise enough to be guided not just by self-interest or popular enthusiasm but by an abiding sense of the principles of right and wrong.

Lecture One
Young Man Lincoln

Scope: The young Abraham Lincoln was born with little more in hand than his own natural talents, but those talents were considerable, especially for talking and for study. His father, Thomas, was more than contented with the life of a classic Jeffersonian farmer in Kentucky, with a strong helping of Calvinistic religion. But the son rebelled against it all—against his father's lack of ambition, his father's farm life, and his father's religion. The Lincolns moved from Kentucky to Indiana in 1816. When the Lincoln family moved from Indiana to Illinois in 1830, Abraham Lincoln struck out on his own for New Salem, Illinois, and a life in commerce, and he never looked back. He served briefly in the Illinois militia in the Black Hawk War of 1832 and made that experience one of the springboards for an entry into state politics.

Outline

I.   Abraham Lincoln was marked from his youth as possessing special talents.

    A. He took naturally to speaking in public.

        1. He loved to tell jokes and stories.

        2. He frequently quoted poetry.

        3. He could mimic sermons.

    B. Abraham's talents irritated and embarrassed his father, Thomas Lincoln.

        1. Thomas Lincoln was descended from Samuel Lincoln of Massachusetts.

        2. The Lincolns had migrated through Pennsylvania and Virginia to Kentucky.

        3. Thomas's father, Abraham, was killed by Indians in Kentucky.

        4. Thomas purchased land in Kentucky but was badgered by defects in land titles.

        5. Thomas Lincoln moved to Indiana in 1816, where his wife, Nancy, died.

6. Thomas remarried to Sarah Bush Johnston, a widow with three children.
7. Abraham adored Sarah but quarreled with his father over education and religion.
8. Thomas Lincoln moved to Illinois in 1830.

II. Once he came of age in 1831, Abraham Lincoln left his father and relocated to New Salem, Illinois, on the Sangamon River.

A. Lincoln's first employment was as a store clerk.
1. He was meticulous in his accounting.
2. He had a reputation for making fun of religion.
3. His favorite reading was Shakespeare and Burns.
4. He won local admiration by wrestling Jack Armstrong to a draw.

B. Lincoln was elected a militia captain in the Black Hawk War, a success from which he gained great satisfaction.
1. Lincoln saw no military action.
2. Nevertheless, he was well admired and made important friends.
3. His election as militia captain gave him great satisfaction throughout his life.

C. Lincoln announced himself as a candidate for the state legislature.
1. He was defeated in 1832 because of time spent on militia duty.
2. He ran again in 1834 and won.
3. He had a rather shrill, monotone style of speaking, but his voice carried well and did not tire; this deficit turned out to be an asset for him during his political career.

Essential Reading:

Thomas, *Lincoln's New Salem*.

Supplementary Reading:

Tarbell, *In the Footsteps of the Lincolns*, chapters 1 through 7.

Warren, *Lincoln's Youth: Indiana Years, 1816–1830*, chapters 4, 8, 13, and 14.

Questions to Consider:

1. What characteristics of the young Lincoln indicate strengths he would later employ as a national leader?
2. How different were Lincoln and his father?

Lecture Two
Whig Meteor

Scope: Lincoln's entry into politics coincided with the emergence of a new national political party, the Whigs, founded by Henry Clay as an opposition party to the dominant American political party, the Democrats, and their chief, Andrew Jackson. Whig political policy was built on three foundations: federal government encouragement for business and finance, social morality and marketplace self-discipline, and the primacy of the national Union over the rights and sovereignty of the individual states. Clay became Lincoln's model and the Whigs his party, and he moved into the forefront of Whig agitation in Illinois for a state bank, state-financed *internal improvements*, and the sale of federal lands to fund the state bank and the state internal improvement projects. His own personal business ventures, however, flopped, and in 1837, he took up the practice of law in Springfield, Illinois.

Outline

I.   Lincoln began his political career with a new political party.

  A. Political parties emerged on the American scene in the 1790s.

   1. One party, the Federalists, was organized around Alexander Hamilton.

   2. The other, the Democratic-Republicans, was organized around Thomas Jefferson.

  B. The War of 1812 raised serious doubts about Democratic policies.

   1. Americans were unprepared and underresourced for the war.

   2. Henry Clay proposed adopting several Hamiltonian policies to compensate.

    a. He called for the refounding of a national bank.

    b. He favored government backing for national transportation projects.

    c. He proposed a national tariff to protect American manufacturing.

  C. The head of the Democratic Party, Andrew Jackson, opposed this proposal.

    1. Jackson vetoed legislation for the Bank of the United States.

    2. Clay declared the formation of a new political party to oppose Jackson, the Whigs.

  D. The Whigs became distinguished for four basic positions.

    1. They opposed Andrew Jackson, whom they accused of being a dictator.

    2. They became the party of small-scale urban business and finance.

    3. They espoused moral issues, including religion, self-discipline, and regularity of behavior.

    4. They believed in the supremacy of the national Union over the individual states.

II. Lincoln's politics as a state legislator reflected the fundamental Whig concerns and interests.

  A. Lincoln promoted an Illinois State Bank that could issue paper money.

    1. The federal government issued as money from its mints only hard coin, known as *specie*.

    2. Paper money was issued by banks.

    3. A state bank would regulate and back up the circulation of paper money.

  B. Lincoln promoted transportation projects (or internal improvements).

    1. Illinois, in 1834, was virtually landlocked.

    2. State funding of internal improvements would open up Illinois to national markets.

  C. Lincoln promoted the sale of public lands.

    1. The capital to fund internal improvements and banks could come only from sales of federally owned public land in Illinois.

    2. Democrats favored keeping the lands to eliminate any excuse for a state bank.

III. Oddly, Lincoln's personal business ventures flopped.

  A. He invested his militia bounty money in a store with William Berry, but the store failed and Lincoln was left seriously in debt.

B. He obtained small jobs to make ends meet.
1. Friends got him the job of postmaster of New Salem.
2. Other friends got him appointed deputy county surveyor.

C. Yet Lincoln remained confident of success and maintained an extraordinary capacity to win friends.
1. He believed he would be a "great man."
2. During the Black Hawk War, he made friends on whom he would rely for the rest of his life, including John Todd Stuart.
3. He began studying law with Stuart, one of the movers and shakers of Illinois politics.

Essential Reading:

Howe, *The Political Culture of the American Whigs*, chapter 11.

Supplementary Reading:

Angle, *Here I Have Lived*, chapters 4 and 5.

Simon, *Lincoln's Preparation for Greatness*, chapters 4 and 6.

Questions to Consider:

1. What were the major elements of Whig political thinking?
2. How did Lincoln's legislative career reflect the larger concerns of the Whig party?

Lecture Three
Lincoln, Law, and Politics

Scope: Lincoln moved directly into professional life as a lawyer, although he was socially awkward and acquired a reputation for religious unbelief. But through the family connections of his law partner, John Todd Stuart, he met and married Mary Todd in 1842 and attached himself to the Whig elite of Springfield, which had become the state capital. He was nominated by the Whigs for Congress in 1846 and won election. His term was undistinguished, and he was unable to parlay his position in Washington into appointive office when a Whig, Zachary Taylor, was elected president in 1848. Lincoln returned to Illinois to face personal difficulties in his family and his own disappointed political ambitions. But he enjoyed substantial success as an attorney, especially in civil litigation with his third law partner, William H. Herndon.

Outline

I. Lincoln's life in Springfield was based around his friendships and his talk.

  A. Lincoln became the center of a "debating society."
  1. He became well known for storytelling.
  2. He acquired a reputation for religious skepticism.

  B. It was through friends that Lincoln was introduced to Mary Todd, John Todd Stuart's cousin.
  1. On the surface, she seemed very different from Lincoln.
  2. In fact, they shared many interests and characteristics.

  C. Lincoln had failed in two earlier romantic forays.
  1. He courted Ann Rutledge in New Salem, but she died in 1835.
  2. He was turned down after proposing to Mary Owens.
  3. He eventually married Mary Todd in 1842.

II. Marriage opened up political connections and opportunities for Lincoln.

A. A new Seventh Congressional District was created around Springfield.

    1. A rotation among Whigs gave the seat first to John Hardin.

    2. In 1846, Lincoln's turn came to run for the seat.

B. The contest hinged on Lincoln's lack of religious identity.

    1. His opponent, Peter Cartwright, accused him of being an "infidel."

    2. Lincoln issued a disclaimer, which reassured voters.

    3. He won, carrying 8 of the 11 counties in the Seventh District.

C. Nevertheless, his tenure in Congress was not a happy one.

    1. Lincoln publicly criticized President Polk for starting the Mexican War.

    2. His request for appointment to federal office was ignored.

D. At home, his troubles increased.

    1. Mary showed signs of mental instability.

    2. Lincoln's second son, Edward, died in 1850.

    3. His father, Thomas, died in 1851.

III. Lincoln's greatest success was in law.

A. Lincoln changed partners three times.

    1. He was John Todd Stuart's junior partner from 1837 to 1841.

    2. He was Stephen T. Logan's junior partner from 1841 to 1844.

    3. He set up his own office and took on William Herndon as a junior partner in 1844.

B. The Lincoln-Herndon case load rose to 400 cases a year, although only five percent was in criminal practice.

    1. Much of the litigation took place in the Eighth Judicial Circuit Courts.

    2. By the 1850s, Lincoln developed a substantial practice in the Illinois Supreme Court and the Federal Circuit Court in Chicago.

    3. Lincoln represented the major Illinois railroad lines.

    4. He earned a healthy income and rebuilt his house.

    5. Despite these successes, Lincoln mourned the seeming death of his political ambitions.

Essential Reading:

Winkle, *The Young Eagle*, chapters 14 through 19.

Supplementary Reading:

Fraysse, *Lincoln, Land and Labor*, chapters 5 and 7.

Riddle, *Lincoln Runs for Congress*.

Questions to Consider:

1. How did Lincoln's religious skepticism threaten his political career?
2. Was Mary Lincoln an asset or a liability for Lincoln's political aspirations?

Lecture Four
The Mind of Abraham Lincoln

Scope: The great legend of Lincoln is that he was the man of the people. But his legendary folksiness overlay a shield Lincoln drew over his inner life and ideas, a shield he rarely, if ever, let down in front of others. The impression many people formed of Lincoln was of an introverted, slightly aloof lawyer who was embarrassed by his lowlife relatives. Still, he disliked wanna-be aristocrats, a resentment that he directed politically at the Democratic Party. He was a tremendous reader and saw no reason why he should not master every subject, from philosophy to political economy, the same way. His preoccupation with honesty was a substitute for religion for Lincoln. He believed in the existence of God, but not the God of Christianity or any other formal religion, though there was never any question in Lincoln's mind that this God was immensely powerful, so powerful that individual human wills really amounted to nothing. Lincoln's fatalism, however, did not make him passive.

Outline

I. Lincoln's personal characteristics clash with much of his legendary image.

    A. Lincoln was ambitious.

        1. He did not wait for the American people to acclaim him.

        2. He became a powerhouse lawyer for the Illinois railroads.

    B. He was secretive and reticent.

        1. His storytelling was a shield to ward off inquisitive snoopers.

        2. He was abstract and absent-minded.

    C. He was embarrassed by any disclosure of his origins.

        1. He liked to stress his success in rising above his origins.

        2. He deeply resented the charge that he had joined the "aristocrats."

        3. He saw Democrats as a wealthy elite who tried to discourage mobility.

D. He preferred logic to emotion.
  1. He was obsessed with clarity of expression.
  2. He was meticulous in preparing cases.

E. One aspect of his personality that does conform to the legend was his honesty.
  1. He warned young lawyers against dishonesty.
  2. He substituted the pursuit of honesty as a replacement for religion.

F. Lincoln's religion resembled the deism of Franklin or Jefferson.
  1. He tended toward *scientific materialism*.
  2. The human will was completely determined in all its choices.
  3. This belief allowed him to pardon or excuse people.
  4. Yet Lincoln was not passive.
  5. Free labor allowed all Americans to make of themselves whatever they were able.

II. Lincoln's anger at slavery grew from its denial of opportunity.

A. The Founders originally expected slavery to pass eventually into oblivion.
  1. The American Revolution dealt slavery a powerful blow.
  2. Slavery was gradually outlawed in the Northern states.

B. The Industrial Revolution's demand for cotton revived slavery.
  1. Cotton became America's most valuable export.
  2. Slave labor was the most efficient means of producing cotton.

C. Lincoln had only incidentally noticed slavery before 1854.
  1. Slavery seemed to pose little threat in Illinois.
  2. This view changed with the renewed attempt of slavery to plant itself in the western territories.

Essential Reading:

Burlingame, *The Inner World of Abraham Lincoln*, chapters 2, 5, and 8.

Supplementary Reading:

Barton, *The Soul of Abraham Lincoln*, chapter 22.

Wilson, *Honor's Voice*, chapter 9.

Questions to Consider:

1. Why was Lincoln a difficult man to understand?
2. What lay at the root of Lincoln's desire to be seen as "honest"?

Lecture Five
Lincoln and Slavery

Scope: Lincoln always detested slavery but never took any serious public stance on the slavery issue before the 1850s. It was inconceivable to Lincoln that slave labor could ever effectively compete with the labor of free men, and he expected that it would naturally die out on its own. But far from fading away, American slavery had been undergoing a tremendous revolution in profitability, based largely on slavery's chief commodity, cotton, in the Southern states of the Union. Slavery sought expansion first in 1819, and the outrage that resulted was quieted only by the Missouri Compromise. Conflict arose again over the admission of Texas in 1845 and the Mexican Cession in 1848, which were quieted by the Compromise of 1850. But in 1854, Illinois Senator Stephen A. Douglas triggered the most lethal round of controversy by junking the Missouri Compromise through the Kansas-Nebraska Act and opening the western territories to slave expansion through the doctrine of *popular sovereignty*. Kansas-Nebraska impelled Lincoln to reenter politics in opposition to slave extension into the territories.

Outline

I.   Lincoln always hated slavery.

    A. Lincoln first protested slavery in public in 1837.

        1. But he made no other important antislavery gestures.

        2. His 1837 protest also condemned abolitionists.

    B. Lincoln believed that slavery was a dying institution.

        1. It ran against the grain of American ideas.

        2. It could not compete with free labor.

    C. Lincoln believed that he had no grounds for interfering with slavery.

        1. The Constitution left decisions about slavery in the hands of the states.

        2. White Northerners had no incentive for interfering with slavery.

        3. Lincoln's Illinois placed severe restrictions on blacks.

        4. Lincoln served as counsel to Robert Matson in an effort to reclaim fugitive slaves.

  D. But slavery was not a dying institution.
        1. Slave labor produced cotton, the nation's greatest export commodity.
        2. Slave productivity was higher than free white labor.
        3. Southern slaveholders were considering moving slave labor into manufacturing.
        4. Supporters of slavery began agitating for expansion of the institution into Missouri in 1819.
        5. They agitated for the annexation of Texas in 1845.
        6. The Mexican War obtained territory that was desired for new slave states.

II. Lincoln principally opposed the expansion of slavery.

  A. Lincoln's opposition to the Mexican War was linked to opposing slavery.
        1. Lincoln believed President Polk wanted war to gain new slave territory.
        2. Lincoln endorsed the Wilmot Proviso, which proposed banning slavery from any territory the United States might win from Mexico.

  B. The controversy over the Mexican Cession was resolved by the Compromise of 1850.
        1. The territories would be allowed to decide for themselves whether they wanted slavery on the basis of popular sovereignty.
        2. The popular sovereignty doctrine was associated with Stephen A. Douglas.

  C. The Compromise of 1850 was so successful in defusing controversy that Douglas proposed to repeal the Missouri Compromise and extend popular sovereignty into the Louisiana Purchase territories.
        1. Douglas introduced the Kansas-Nebraska Bill in 1854.
        2. Lincoln was alarmed by the possibility that Kansas-Nebraska would open those territories to slavery.

D. Lincoln spoke against Douglas in the fall of 1854.
   1. The Founding Fathers always recognized that slavery was an evil.
   2. They wrote the Constitution with the view that slavery would gradually be eliminated.
   3. Southerners could not argue that this was unfair to their property because slaves were human beings, not property.
   4. Slavery was a moral wrong that violated natural law.
   5. But Lincoln would not demand the outright abolition of slavery.
   E. The Illinois legislative elections in 1854 sent Douglas Democrats reeling.
   1. Lincoln offered himself as a candidate for the U.S. Senate.
   2. Democrats closed ranks and elected Lyman Trumbull instead.
   3. Lincoln gradually decided to align himself with the Republicans.

Essential Reading:

Boritt, *The Lincoln Enigma*, chapter 6.

Supplementary Reading:

Carwardine, *Lincoln*, chapter 1.

Miller, *Lincoln's Virtues*, chapter 10.

Questions to Consider:

1. What were the roots of Lincoln's opposition to slavery?
2. Why did Lincoln oppose popular sovereignty?

Lecture Six
The Great Debates

Scope: Kansas-Nebraska and the Supreme Court's denial of restrictions on slavery in the territories galvanized Lincoln to join the Republican Party and challenge Stephen A. Douglas for the Illinois senate seat in 1858. The two candidates engaged in a series of seven open-air debates across Illinois in which Douglas sought to portray Lincoln as an abolitionist fanatic, and Lincoln replied by condemning Douglas's stupendous indifference to the moral wrong of slavery by allowing slavery to spread into Kansas and the other western territories. Lincoln narrowly lost the election but gained national attention that he would soon use to put himself into the presidential running for 1860.

Outline

I.   The Republican Party was a coalition.

    A. The core of the party was old antislavery Whigs, such as Lincoln.

    B. They were supplemented by anti-Nebraska Democrats who felt betrayed by their party.

    C. The party included some abolitionists who wanted slavery destroyed rather than merely restricted.

    D. It was united by the conviction that the South had gone back on a national bargain.

        1. For the South, the bargain included tolerance and noninterference with slavery in the Southern states where it was legal.

        2. For the North, the bargain was an agreement not to expand or extend slavery.

    E. Instead, a *Slave Power* had seized control of the federal government.

        1. It relied on extra representation through the $3/5^{ths}$ clause.

        2. It relied on Southern control of the Democratic Party.

        3. It relied on influence in the federal executive and judiciary.

        4. It would guarantee that slavery would not only rule the territories, but it would also bring slave labor into the mills and factories of the North.

   F. Proof of the existence of the Slave Power came with *Dred Scott v. Sandford*.

        1. Dred Scott sued for his freedom on the grounds that he had been taken by his master into the free territory of Minnesota.

        2. The Supreme Court rejected Scott's suit because he was a black man.

        3. The Supreme Court also ruled that the federal territories could not bar slaveholders.

II. Lincoln got his chance to strike at Douglas and popular sovereignty in 1858.

   A. Lincoln asked for a statewide Republican convention to endorse him for the race against Douglas for the Illinois senate seat.

        1. Lincoln used his acceptance speech to describe the United States as a "house divided."

        2. This was not intended as a radical statement but was interpreted as such.

   B. In July, Lincoln challenged Douglas to a series of seven debates.

        1. Douglas portrayed Lincoln in the first debate as an abolitionist radical.

        2. Lincoln replied in the second debate by pointing out the contradiction between popular sovereignty and the *Dred Scott* decision.

        3. In the fourth debate, Lincoln denied the charge of promoting racial equality but defended natural equality.

        4. In the last three debates, Lincoln attacked Douglas as a moral fiend.

   C. Republicans failed to gain a majority in the Illinois legislature.

        1. Douglas was reelected on a party-line vote.

        2. But Lincoln gained national attention as a comer in the Republican ranks.

Essential Reading:

Jaffa, *Crisis of the House Divided*, chapters 15 and 16.

Supplementary Reading:

Fehrenbacher, *Prelude to Greatness*, chapters 5 and 6.

Sigelshiffer, *The American Conscience*, chapter 14.

Questions to Consider:

1. How could Lincoln reconcile his belief in the *natural* equality of all people but claim not to support the *civil* equality of blacks and whites?

2. What were Lincoln's principal arguments against Douglas in the debates of 1858?

Lecture Seven
Lincoln and Liberty, Too

Scope: Lincoln dismissed much of the talk he heard of a presidential nomination, but it was less farfetched than he realized. The Democrats went into the 1860 election bitterly divided, and the Republican frontrunners had compromised themselves with too much antislavery radicalism. After successfully impressing East Coast Republicans with a major address at New York's Cooper Institute, Lincoln's backers stage-managed his nomination at the Republican national convention in May 1860. In an effort to avoid controversy, Lincoln declined to comment on Southern threats to secede from the Union and managed to win the presidency by garnering almost all the electoral votes of the North.

Outline

I. The 1858 debates made Lincoln nationally known.

    A. Lincoln was showered with invitations for speaking engagements.

        1. He spoke on agricultural policy to the Wisconsin State Agricultural Fair.

        2. He campaigned in Ohio on behalf of Salmon Chase.

        3. In February 1860, he was invited to speak at New York City's Cooper Institute.

    B. Lincoln at first dismissed all talk that this newfound celebrity would lead to a presidential nomination.

        1. There were other better-known Republican candidates.

        2. The Republicans were a minority party, and Lincoln had already lost as a minority-party candidate.

    C. But talk of the nomination was not that farfetched.

        1. The Republicans had done surprisingly well in 1856.

        2. The Democrats were divided by Southerners who had panicked over John Brown's raid.

        3. If the Republicans picked a candidate who stressed moderation, they might win the White House in 1860.

    D. Lincoln began his own push for the nomination with the Cooper Institute address.

1. He declared that the Founders anticipated the gradual disappearance of slavery.
2. Republicans were not plotting some violent, forcible end to slavery.
3. Lincoln added, however, that Republicans would not permit the spread of slavery into the territories.

E. The key to a successful presidential nomination depended on two things.
1. Location: Lincoln's friends brought the nominating convention to Chicago.
2. Electability: Lincoln's friends painted the other candidates as unacceptable.

F. Lincoln was nominated on the third ballot.

II. Lincoln's nomination came as a surprise.

A. People did not even know what he looked like.
1. Artists had to be hired to reinvent his image.
2. He eventually grew a beard to emphasize his sober eldership.

B. The inevitability of Democratic defeat threw the South into a frenzy.
1. Southerners concluded that Lincoln's election would be the signal for slave rebellion.
2. At best, a Lincoln presidency would mean the end of any new slave states.

C. Lincoln did little to assuage these fears.
1. He did not begin a formal campaign.
2. He declined to issue statements.
3. He did not really believe that the South was serious about threats of secession.

D. Lincoln was elected president on November 6, 1860.
1. He garnered 1.8 million popular votes and 180 electoral votes.
2. Four days later, the state legislature of South Carolina called for a secession convention.

Essential Reading:
Donald, *Lincoln*, chapter 9.

Supplementary Reading:

Holzer, *Lincoln at Cooper Union*, chapter 6.

Leech, *Reveille in Washington*, chapter 3.

Questions to Consider:

1. What factors stood in the path of a Lincoln nomination in 1860?

2. Was there any argument Lincoln could have used to persuade the South not to secede?

Lecture Eight
The Uncertain President

Scope: South Carolina led the Southern states in seceding from the Union and forming an independent Confederate States of America. It was not clear that Lincoln had the experience or the skill to manage this situation, and his offers of conciliation fell on deaf ears in the South. The Confederates attempted to evict federal troops from military installations in the South and finally bombarded one of them, Fort Sumter, into submission. Lincoln could not avoid this challenge: He regarded secession as illegal and a constitutional impossibility, and he responded to the attack on Sumter by calling out the militia of the states. He hoped that one single military stroke would cow the Southerners, but the first battle of the Civil War, at Bull Run, was a defeat for the Union army. Lincoln then turned to George McClellan as his chief strategist and aimed to secure the Border States, divide the Confederacy militarily, and keep any dealings with slavery on a separate political track.

Outline

I. By the time Lincoln was inaugurated, Southern states had organized the Confederate States of America.

   A. Lincoln seemed to be lacking in experience for managing this situation.
      1. Lincoln had been a successful lawyer, but he had never been a governor or a mayor and had never administered anything larger than his law practice.
      2. He tried to placate party leaders by putting his rivals, Seward and Chase, into the cabinet.
      3. Even inside his own office, Lincoln seemed disorganized.

   B. Lincoln tried to stem secession in his inaugural address.
      1. He promised to oppose any new extension of slavery.
      2. He would not, however, interfere with slavery in the Southern states.
      3. He pleaded with the Southern states to rethink their rash actions.

C. Instead, the Confederates seized federal property and installations in the South.
    1. They isolated Fort Sumter in Charleston harbor.
    2. On April 12, 1861, they bombarded it.

II. Lincoln called on the loyal states for 75,000 of the states' militia.

A. The upper South protested.
    1. Tennessee, North Carolina, and Virginia joined the Confederacy.
    2. In Maryland, Kentucky, and Missouri, the political tension was high.

B. The federal army was defeated at Bull Run.

C. Lincoln then called on George Brinton McClellan to organize a strategy that included the following:
    1. Secure the Border States (Maryland, Delaware, Kentucky, and Missouri).
    2. Divide the Confederacy by driving from Kentucky into eastern Tennessee, launching into Virginia, and landing an offensive along the Carolina coast.
    3. Downplay any mention of freeing slaves.

D. Much of this strategy seemed, at first, to work.
    1. McClellan organized the Army of the Potomac.
    2. In August 1861, the federal navy seized control of the Hatteras Sound area.
    3. Ulysses S. Grant captured Fort Henry and Fort Donelson.

E. But there was less real agreement between Lincoln and McClellan than it seemed.

Essential Reading:

Potter, *Lincoln and His Party in the Secession Crisis*, chapter 12.

Supplementary Reading:

Hendrick, *Lincoln's War Cabinet*, chapter 1.

Jaffa, *New Birth of Freedom*, chapters 4 and 5.

Questions to Consider:

1. Why was Lincoln at first regarded as inadequate and uncertain in the presidency?

2. What was Lincoln's original strategy for suppressing the rebellion in 1861?

Lecture Nine
The Emancipation Moment

Scope: General McClellan was a great organizer but strategically lethargic. He was soon at odds with Congress over his indifference to slavery and with Lincoln over the best way to win the war. Only after direct prodding from Lincoln did McClellan undertake a campaign against the Confederate capital, Richmond, in May 1862, and that campaign bogged down in failure. Lincoln eventually concluded that he had no choice but to connect the war with the ending of slavery, over McClellan's opposition. Lincoln's original plan for the emancipation of the slaves had been to offer gradual buyouts, but when these were refused by the Border States, he turned to emancipation by military decree, through the Emancipation Proclamation.

Outline

I. Although General McClellan was a great organizer, he caused people to quickly grow impatient that there was no forward movement of the army.

   A. That impatience was felt most keenly of all in Congress.
   1. The Thirty-seventh Congress held a Republican majority.
   2. The leading edge of that majority was Radical Republicans.
   3. The Radicals formed a Joint Committee on the Conduct of the War.
   4. Some members called on Lincoln to replace McClellan.

   B. McClellan responded to criticism with contempt.

   C. When McClellan became ill, Lincoln tried to intervene.
   1. He queried commanders, asking for information and proposals.
   2. He suggested taking personal command of the Army of the Potomac.
   3. Lincoln issued General War Order #1.

   D. McClellan proposed to invade Virginia via the James River peninsula, and Lincoln authorized the proposal on two conditions.
   1. McClellan's army would be reorganized into four army corps.

      2. One army corps would remain in Washington to guard the city.

II. McClellan's campaign to the peninsula went disastrously awry.

    A. McClellan took fright at the slightest sign of Confederate resistance.

        1. This gave the main Confederate army time to fall back to Richmond.

        2. McClellan believed the Confederates had 200,000 men.

        3. He permitted Robert E. Lee to take the offensive.

    B. In the Seven Days battles, McClellan was driven back from Richmond.

    C. After that humiliating series of defeats, an unembarrassed McClellan presented Lincoln with a letter warning against emancipation.

III. Lincoln's notion of emancipation was originally separate from the war.

    A. Lincoln believed that any emancipation plan had three features:

        1. It should be on a timetable.

        2. It should involve the payment of compensation to the slaveowners.

        3. It should be approved by the people.

    B. He was ready to entice the Border States into instituting emancipation themselves.

        1. In November 1861, Lincoln drew up a plan for Delaware.

        2. In March 1862, he endorsed compensation for the other Border States.

        3. The Border States refused the offer.

        4. Lincoln also had to deal with the possibility that McClellan might stage some form of military intervention.

    C. On July 22, 1862, Lincoln unveiled an emancipation proclamation to the cabinet.

        1. It abandoned attempts at gradualism.

        2. He claimed this constituted an exercise of his war powers.

        3. He proclaimed the slaves *forever free*.

        4. Secretary Seward persuaded him to await a federal military victory.

D. Lincoln struggled to discern emancipation as part of the will of God.

    1. When Lee was defeated at Antietam, Lincoln believed this Union victory was a sign from God.

    2. On September 22, 1862, Lincoln made the Emancipation Proclamation official.

Essential Reading:

Cox, *Lincoln and Black Freedom*, chapter 1.

Supplementary Reading:

Carwardine, *Lincoln*, chapter 5.

Pinsker, *Lincoln's Sanctuary: Abraham Lincoln and the Soldiers' Home*, chapter 3.

Questions to Consider:

1. What were the three components of Lincoln's original plan for emancipation?

2. Why did Lincoln change this plan and move to an emancipation proclamation in 1862?

Lecture Ten
Lincoln's Triumph

Scope: The Emancipation Proclamation cost Lincoln and his party dearly at the polls in the 1862 off-year Congressional elections. He also sustained deep personal wounds in the death of his son, Willie, and in Mary Lincoln's extravagant behavior. His cabinet proved divided and uncooperative, and the Radical members of his own party in Congress agitated for more extreme gestures against slavery. At the same time, congressional Democrats stiffened their opposition to his administration and a Democratic chief justice of the Supreme Court sought legal monkey wrenches to throw into his administration's works. But Lincoln drew on his confidence in the will of God and his shrewd powers of analysis of both people and situations to steer himself through these crises; he eventually won the respect of even the most jaded observers.

Outline

I. The war and the Emancipation Proclamation threatened the survival of Lincoln's administration.

    A. Republicans were badly bruised in the 1862 elections.

        1. In Illinois, Republicans lost control of both houses of the legislature.

        2. In Congress, Republicans held onto majorities in the House and Senate.

    B. Lincoln replaced McClellan with Ambrose Burnside.

        1. Burnside led the army to a defeat at Fredericksburg.

        2. Joseph Hooker led soldiers to another defeat at Chancellorsville.

    C. Lincoln also had to deal with personal losses.

        1. Mary Lincoln was disrespected in Washington society.

        2. His son, William Wallace Lincoln ("Willie"), died in February 1862.

    D. Lincoln even lacked support within his party.

        1. Seward and Chase were eager to take control.

        2. Radicals chaired the committees in Congress.

- **E.** The Democratic opposition recovered its wind.
    - **1.** In Congress, Democrats recovered seats in the 1862 election.
    - **2.** Chief Justice Taney obstructed the war effort through decisions in *ex parte Merryman* and *Prize Cases*.
- **II.** But Lincoln had resources to call on for strength.
    - **A.** He always believed in predestination.
        - **1.** If all events were preordained, his task was simply to see that they were carried out.
        - **2.** This conviction strengthened him past all the opposition and criticism of emancipation.
    - **B.** Lincoln possessed shrewd powers of analysis of others' strengths and weaknesses.
        - **1.** He outmaneuvered the Radicals in Congress over Secretary Seward.
        - **2.** He pocket-vetoed the Wade-Davis Bill.
    - **C.** Onlookers noted a substantial growth in Lincoln's presidential abilities.
        - **1.** He impressed others with his improved executive ability and his intelligence.
        - **2.** He learned to deal better with his cabinet members.
        - **3.** He learned how to influence others rather than be influenced by them.

Essential Reading:

Paludan, *The Presidency of Abraham Lincoln*, chapters 8 and 12.

Supplementary Reading:

Carpenter, *Six Months in the White House with Abraham Lincoln*.

Hendrick, *Lincoln's War Cabinet*, chapter 5.

Questions to Consider:

1. How did the Supreme Court emerge as an obstacle for Lincoln?
2. What role did Lincoln's belief in predestination play in his presidency?

Lecture Eleven
The President's Sword

Scope: Among Lincoln's greatest personal assets was his persuasiveness as a writer, and he was able to win support for his administration through his mastery of argument in his great inaugural addresses, occasional speeches at significant public events (for example, the Gettysburg Address), and his public letters. Lincoln used both speeches and letters as a way of being his own best defender of his ideas, and his success was extraordinary. Lincoln's gift for winning cases was matched by the gift for battlefield victory offered by Ulysses S. Grant, whom Lincoln promoted to supreme command of the Union armies in 1864. Even Grant, however, was able to achieve little more than a siege of Richmond, and by the summer of 1864, Lincoln was fearful that he would be defeated for reelection that fall. But a string of Union military victories rejuvenated Lincoln's fortunes, and he was easily reelected over the Democratic nominee, his former general, George McClellan.

Outline

I. One of Lincoln's greatest assets was his skill as a communicator.

   A. The lessons he learned during the daily experience of practicing law were the most important influence on his writing and speaking style.
      1. Precision and brevity were key to winning cases.
      2. Compulsive speechmaking alienates a jury.

   B. His most important *live* speeches were the following:
      1. His two great inaugural addresses
      2. The occasional speech he would deliver at a public event (such as the Gettysburg Address).

   C. Lincoln also mastered the art of the public letter.
      1. Lincoln's most famous public letter was written to Horace Greeley on emancipation.
      2. He also wrote public letters to Erastus Corning and the Democrats of New York and called for a statewide Republican rally in Springfield, Illinois, in August 1863.

II. Lincoln matched his superb assets as a communicator with the great asset of a victorious general, Ulysses S. Grant.

    A. Grant had won significant victories in the West.

        1. He had seized Forts Henry and Donelson in 1862.

        2. He had forced the surrender of Vicksburg in 1863.

    B. But Grant was dogged by rumors of character flaws.

        1. People believed he was an alcoholic.

        2. He had been caught by surprise at Shiloh.

    C. Grant justified himself in Lincoln's eyes by the victory at Chattanooga.

        1. Congress revived the army rank of lieutenant general.

        2. Grant was persuaded to take charge in the East.

III. The campaigns of 1864 began well but almost ended badly.

    A. Grant invaded Virginia.

        1. He was stunned by the ferocity of rebel resistance at the Wilderness.

        2. He became bogged down in a siege at Petersburg.

    B. William T. Sherman invaded Georgia.

        1. Joseph Johnston delayed Sherman's advance.

        2. Sherman also became bogged down in a siege of Atlanta.

    C. McClellan was nominated for the presidency by the Democrats.

        1. McClellan promised an immediate armistice.

        2. Democrats were exultant at prospects for success.

    D. By the fall, the fortunes of war changed dramatically.

        1. Sherman captured Atlanta.

        2. The Confederate commerce raider *Alabama* was sunk.

        3. Union Admiral David Farragut closed Mobile, Alabama.

    E. Lincoln won a crushing 55 percent of the popular vote.

Essential Reading:

Donald, *Lincoln*, chapters 18 and 19.

Supplementary Reading:

Klement, *The Gettysburg Soldiers' Cemetery and Lincoln's Address*, chapter 6.

Warren, *Lincoln's Gettysburg Declaration*, chapters 12 and 13.

Questions to Consider:

1. Why did Lincoln hesitate over Ulysses Grant, and what made him change his mind?

2. What was the public letter, and how did Lincoln use it in 1863?

Lecture Twelve
The Dream of Lincoln

Scope: Over the winter of 1864–1865, the Confederate cause began to collapse on itself. Lincoln insisted that he had no single plan for reconstructing the defeated South, and he preferred to let the Southern states sort out their own wreckage and rejoin the Union as quickly as possible. In his Second Inaugural Address, Lincoln offered a quasi theology of the war, rebuking Radicals of his own party who were planning a vengeful reconstruction of the South. But Lincoln was already beginning to attach conditions to reconstruction himself, beginning with recognition of slave emancipation and conferral of voting rights on freed slaves. These plans were cut short by Lincoln's murder at Ford's Theater on the night of April 14, 1865, by John Wilkes Booth. But Lincoln left a long-term legacy that affirmed the opportunities of an open society, the primacy of the idea of equality of natural rights for all, and the necessity of retaining moral content in the decisions made by popular democracies.

Outline

I. Lincoln's reelection was interpreted as a defeat for the Confederacy.

    A. Large portions of the Confederacy were under Union occupation:
        1. All of the Mississippi River valley;
        2. Virtually all of Tennessee and Arkansas;
        3. All of the major Southern ports except for Charleston and Wilmington, North Carolina.

    B. The means for supporting the rebel armies were shrinking.
        1. Confederate armies began to hemorrhage deserters.
        2. Southern states demanded peace talks with the North.

    C. Jefferson Davis dispatched emissaries to meet with Lincoln.

    D. Lee endorsed the recruiting and arming of black slaves.

II. Lincoln now turned his attention to the postwar settlement.

    A. He preferred to let the defeated states rejoin the Union as quickly as possible.

1. He insisted on abolition of slavery and ratification of the Thirteenth Amendment.
2. He preferred that Confederate leaders quietly disappear into exile.
3. He wanted to keep the Radicals of his own party at bay.

B. In his Second Inaugural Address, Lincoln offered a philosophical interpretation of the war.
1. The war was clearly about slavery.
2. But God intended it as a judgment on the whole nation.
3. The best response was humility—malice toward none, charity for all.

C. The Confederacy collapsed in the spring of 1865.
1. Lee surrendered at Appomattox.
2. Sherman cornered the other Confederate army in North Carolina.

D. Lincoln hoped for quick readjustment.
1. He deplored preoccupation with theoretical and legal niceties.
2. But he also urged awarding full civil rights to blacks.
3. He expected good news from Sherman.

E. Lincoln attended the theater on April 14, 1865.
1. He was shot there by John Wilkes Booth, an actor and sometime secret Confederate agent.
2. Lincoln died the next morning.

III. The great achievement of Abraham Lincoln was his reaffirmation of constitutional democracy.

A. He gave a lifelong demonstration of the openness of American society.
1. He believed in a society based on rights, not status.
2. If ever anyone believed in the American Dream, it was Lincoln.

B. He was devoted to the statement of the Declaration of Independence about equality.
1. Lincoln took equality of rights as a universal feature of human nature.
2. He distinguished equality of rights from equality of outcomes.

    C. Lincoln closely bonded political and moral considerations.
        1. Politics must conform to the eternal principles of right and wrong.
        2. The future must be seen under the dictates of the justice of God.

Essential Reading:

Boritt, *Lincoln and the Economics of the American Dream*, chapter 19.

Supplementary Reading:

Harris, *Lincoln's Last Months*, chapter 8.

Lewis, *Myths after Lincoln*, chapters 5 through 7.

Questions to Consider:

1. What did Lincoln's plans for the postwar South involve?
2. How did Lincoln manage to blend politics and morality?

Timeline

February 12, 1809 .... Abraham Lincoln is born near Hodgenville, Kentucky, second child of Thomas and Nancy Hanks Lincoln.

Autumn/winter 1816 .... Lincoln family moves to Spencer County, Indiana.

October 5, 1818 .... Lincoln's mother, Nancy Hanks Lincoln, dies.

December 2, 1819 .... Lincoln's father, Thomas, remarries to Sarah Bush Johnston.

February 16, 1820 .... Missouri Compromise is adopted.

January 14, 1824 .... Henry Clay begins exposition of the *American System* before Congress.

March 1, 1830 .... The Lincoln family again uproots and moves to central Illinois.

July 1831 .... Lincoln takes up residence in New Salem, Illinois.

April 7, 1832 .... Lincoln is elected captain of a company in the Thirty-first Illinois Militia.

April 14, 1834 .... Henry Clay applies the term *Whig* to the anti-Jackson opposition.

August 4, 1834 .... Lincoln is elected to the Illinois state legislature.

March 3, 1837 .... With Dan Stone, Lincoln enters protest against the injustice of slavery in Illinois legislature.

April 15, 1837 .... Lincoln begins law practice with John Todd Stuart in Springfield.

April 4, 1841 .... President William Henry Harrison, the first Whig president, becomes the first president to die in office.

November 4, 1842 .... Lincoln marries Mary Todd.

August 1, 1843 .... Robert Todd Lincoln, the Lincolns' first child, is born.

March 10, 1846 .... Edward Baker Lincoln, the Lincolns' second son, is born.

May 11/12, 1846 .... Congress approves President Polk's request for a declaration of war, beginning the Mexican War.

August 3, 1846 .... Lincoln is elected to represent the Illinois Seventh District in the Thirtieth Congress.

February 2, 1848 .... Treaty of Guadalupe Hidalgo ends the Mexican War and provides for cession of 500,000 square miles to the United States.

January 29, 1850 .... Henry Clay introduces the bills that are to shape the Compromise of 1850.

February 1, 1850 .... Edward Baker Lincoln dies after a 52-day illness.

December 21, 1850 .... William Wallace ("Willie") Lincoln, the Lincolns' third son, is born.

January 17, 1851 .... Lincoln's father, Thomas, dies in Coles County, Illinois.

June 1, 1851 .... *The National Era* begins serialization of a new novel about slavery by Harriet Beecher Stowe, *Uncle Tom's Cabin, or Life among the Lowly*.

April 4, 1853 .... Thomas ("Tad") Lincoln, the Lincolns' fourth son, is born.

January 4, 1854 .... Stephen A. Douglas reports a bill for the organization of the Kansas and Nebraska territories, setting aside the Missouri Compromise and permitting

	inhabitants of the territories to decide for themselves on slavery.
October 4, 1854	Lincoln speaks in opposition to Stephen A. Douglas at the Illinois State Fair in Springfield on the Kansas-Nebraska Act.
October 16, 1854	Lincoln speaks in opposition to Douglas at Peoria, Illinois, on the Kansas-Nebraska Act.
February 8, 1855	Lincoln is defeated in his bid for election to the U.S. Senate by the Illinois legislature.
February 22, 1856	Lincoln meets with antislavery Illinois newspaper editors to issue a call for a state Republican organizing convention in Bloomington, Illinois.
May 29, 1856	Lincoln delivers the keynote speech to the convention in Bloomington.
March 6, 1857	United States Supreme Court hands down the decision in *Dred Scott v. Sandford*, denying that Congress has the power to bar slavery from the territories or that blacks have citizenship rights.
December 8, 1857	President Buchanan endorses the proslavery Lecompton Constitution for Kansas Territory.
June 16, 1858	Lincoln is nominated unanimously to run for the U.S. Senate by the Illinois Republican Party and delivers the House Divided speech.
August 2, 1858	Kansas voters reject the proslavery Lecompton Constitution.

August 21–October 15, 1858	Lincoln participates in a series of seven debates with Stephen A. Douglas.
October 17, 1859	John Brown's raid on Harpers Ferry takes place.
February 27, 1860	Lincoln delivers his Cooper Institute address in New York City.
May 18, 1860	Lincoln is nominated for president by the Republican National Convention in Chicago.
November 6, 1860	Lincoln is elected, defeating Stephen A. Douglas, John Breckinridge, and John Bell.
December 20, 1860	South Carolina secedes from the Union.
February 8, 1861	Constitution for the Confederate States of America is adopted in Montgomery, Alabama.
March 4, 1861	Lincoln is inaugurated as the 16th president of the United States.
April 15, 1861	After the attack on Fort Sumter, Lincoln issues a proclamation, calling on states to provide 75,000 militia to suppress the rebellion.
July 21, 1861	Union suffers defeat at the First Battle of Bull Run.
July 22, 1861	George B. McClellan is called to Washington to take command of federal troops.
February 20, 1862	William Wallace ("Willie") Lincoln dies.
April 5–July 3, 1862	McClellan's Peninsular Campaign takes place.

July 22, 1862	Lincoln reads first draft of the Emancipation Proclamation to his cabinet.
August 29–30, 1862	Union is defeated at the Second Battle of Bull Run.
September 17, 1862	McClellan defeats Lee at the Battle of Antietam.
September 22, 1862	Lincoln presents the preliminary Emancipation Proclamation to his cabinet.
November 7, 1862	Lincoln relieves McClellan of command of the Army of the Potomac.
December 13, 1862	Union suffers costly defeat at the Battle of Fredericksburg.
January 1, 1863	Lincoln signs Emancipation Proclamation.
May 1–3, 1863	Union is defeated at the Battle of Chancellorsville.
July 1–3, 1863	Union wins the Battle of Gettysburg.
July 4, 1863	Vicksburg surrenders to Grant.
September 3, 1863	Lincoln's letter to the Springfield Union meeting is read aloud.
November 19, 1863	Lincoln delivers the dedicatory remarks at the Soldiers' National Cemetery at Gettysburg; those remarks later become known as the Gettysburg Address.
May–June, 1864	Grant wages the Overland Campaign, ending in the siege of Richmond.
September 2, 1864	Atlanta falls to Sherman.
November 8, 1864	Lincoln is reelected president.

March 4, 1865 .... Lincoln is inaugurated for his second presidential term.

April 9, 1865 .... Lee surrenders to Grant at Appomattox.

April 14, 1865 .... Lincoln is assassinated in Ford's Theater by John Wilkes Booth and dies at 7:22 the next morning.

April 26, 1865 .... Booth is apprehended and shot to death by federal cavalry in Virginia.

May 4, 1865 .... Lincoln's funeral takes place in Springfield, Illinois.

July 7, 1865 .... Four principal conspirators in the Lincoln assassination are hanged.

July 15, 1871 .... "Tad" Lincoln dies in Chicago.

July 16, 1882 .... Mary Todd Lincoln dies in Springfield.

May 30, 1922 .... The Lincoln Memorial in Washington, DC, is dedicated.

July 26, 1926 .... Robert Todd Lincoln dies at his estate, Hildene, in Vermont.

July 26, 1947 .... Lincoln's presidential papers are opened to the public at the Library of Congress.

Glossary

Abolitionism: A movement that gathered public visibility beginning in the 1830s; dedicated to the immediate and complete abolition of slavery in the United States.

Antietam: Site of the Union victory in Maryland on September 17, 1862, which allowed Lincoln to move forward to issue the Emancipation Proclamation on September 22nd.

Antislavery: The larger segment of opinion that opposed slavery but not necessarily through immediate abolition.

Appomattox Court House: Site chosen for the meeting of Ulysses S. Grant and Robert E. Lee to arrange the surrender of Lee's army, April 9, 1865.

Army of the Potomac: The principal Union field army in the eastern theater of the Civil War, originally organized and commanded by George B. McClellan and commanded afterward by Ambrose Burnside, Joseph Hooker, and George G. Meade.

Black Hawk War: Begun in 1832 by Sauk and Fox Indians as a means of reclaiming lands in northern Illinois and put down by federal troops and Illinois militia (in which Lincoln commanded a company).

Bull Run: Northern Virginia site of two Union defeats in the Civil War, in July 1861 and August 1862.

Calvinism: A system of religious doctrine developed by John Calvin that taught the unlimited sovereignty and power of God in ordering all human affairs.

Chancellorsville: Major Union defeat in central Virginia in May 1863 by Robert E. Lee.

Chattanooga: Major Union victory in November 1863 under the command of Ulysses S. Grant.

Chickamauga: Major Union defeat in September 1863 under William S. Rosecrans, leading to Confederate siege of the Union forces in Chattanooga until relieved by Ulysses S. Grant.

Cold Harbor: Union defeat north of Richmond in June 1864 as part of Ulysses S. Grant's Overland Campaign.

Compromise of 1850: A settlement devised by Henry Clay and steered through Congress by Stephen A. Douglas that allowed for a peaceful organization of the Mexican Cession but widely regarded as a sellout to the Slave Power by antislavery interests.

Copperhead: Term of mockery attached by Republicans during the Civil War to antiwar Democrats, comparing them to snakes who struck without warning.

Deism: A general term describing a religion based on rational deduction from the evidences of nature of the existence and attributes of a supreme deity, rather than from an authoritative supernatural revelation.

Democrat: Term for the political party begun as the Democratic-Republicans under Jefferson that became the vehicle for expressing the political attitudes and culture symbolized by Andrew Jackson.

***Dred Scott v. Sanford* (1857)**: Decision of the U.S. Supreme Court written by Chief Justice Taney, denying that Dred Scott, a slave, had standing to sue for his freedom or that Congress had the power to forbid the extension of slavery into the territories.

Fatalism: Philosophical idea that all events are caused so as to allow no resistance by individuals to their occurring and without any exercise of free will.

Ford's Theater: Originally built as a Baptist church on 10th Street in Washington, DC, but converted to a theater in 1862 by John Ford. Lincoln was assassinated there on April 14, 1865, by John Wilkes Booth, while watching a performance of *Our American Cousin*.

Fort Donelson: Site of Ulysses S. Grant's first major victory in the war, capturing a key Confederate fort in Tennessee in February 1862.

Fort Sumter: The initial battle of the Civil War, in which Confederate and South Carolina forces bombarded the federal garrison in Fort Sumter into surrender on April 14, 1861.

Fredericksburg: Central Virginia site of Union defeat in December 1862, as the Army of the Potomac, under Ambrose Burnside, attempted to force its way past the Confederate army, under Robert E. Lee.

Free labor: Economic system in which an individual, protected by natural and civil rights, is free to seek terms of employment, looks for pay in the form of cash wages, and may accumulate sufficient capital through work and savings to acquire property and hire others.

Gettysburg: Union victory won by the Army of the Potomac on July 1–3, 1863. The first national military cemetery was laid out there and dedicated on November 19, 1863, with Lincoln delivering the dedication remarks that became known as the Gettysburg Address.

Habeas corpus (literally, "to have the body"): The so-called Great Writ that allows a judge to demand the release of prisoners from imprisonment for trial, thus preventing arbitrary arrest and detention by a government. It can be suspended in time of war, insurrection, or other national emergency. Lincoln's suspension of the writ in 1861 was the occasion for Chief Justice Taney's attempt to restrict Lincoln's presidential powers in *ex parte Merryman*.

Harrison's Landing: Encampment chosen on the James River by George McClellan as the point of concentration for the Union army as it retreated from the Peninsula Campaign. McClellan wrote his Harrison's Landing Letter on Union slave policy when Lincoln visited the army there in July 1862.

House Divided Speech (June 16, 1858): Lincoln's acceptance speech on, at the Illinois state Republican convention, which had nominated him as the Republican candidate for the U.S. Senate against Stephen A. Douglas.

Illinois State Bank: Created to fund internal improvements in Illinois and supported by Lincoln as a Whig state legislator; failed after Jackson's "Bank War" and the Panic of 1837.

Industrial Revolution: The introduction of machine-based and steam-powered means of production, which recruited large numbers of the rural population as a workforce, making cities the central points of commercial exchange and wage labor the principal means of compensating workers.

Internal improvements: Refers to federal government sponsorship for building up the economic infrastructure; favored principally by the Whig Party as a component of Henry Clay's American System.

Joint Committee on the Conduct of the War: Organized by Radical Republicans in the Thirty-seventh Congress as a means for reviewing the military performance of the Union armies and prodding Union generals into more energetic movements against the Confederacy.

Kansas-Nebraska Bill (1854): Crafted by Stephen A. Douglas as the enabling legislation in Congress for the organization of Kansas and Nebraska as federal territories and specifically permitting use of popular sovereignty as the means for determining the legality of slavery in both.

Lincoln-Douglas debates: Series of seven debates held between Lincoln and Stephen A. Douglas (on Lincoln's challenge) from August to October 1858 as part of Douglas's campaign for reelection to the U.S. Senate.

Matson v. Rutherford **(1847)**: Suit brought by Robert Matson against an Illinois abolitionist, Hiram Rutherford, for damages sustained through Rutherford's attempt to help Matson's slaves escape from his control while they were working Matson's farm in Illinois. Matson retained Lincoln as counsel in the suit.

Mexican Cession: The lands ceded by Mexico to the United States as part of the settlement that ended the Mexican War (comprising California, New Mexico, Arizona, Nevada, and Colorado).

Mexican War: Fought by the United States and Mexico (1846–1848) as part of President Polk's program of national expansion but opposed by Lincoln and Whigs who feared that it was a device for obtaining new lands for the expansion of slavery.

Missouri Compromise (1820): Measure crafted by Henry Clay that permitted the admission to the Union of Missouri as a slave state and Maine as a free state, thereby defusing the first major confrontation over slavery in Congress.

Natural law: Refers to the general understanding that certain moral principles are inherently present in human thinking and are universally self-evident to all people, as distinct from *positive law*, which described the legal arrangements individual societies make for their own governance (although positive law is understood to need guidance from natural law to function appropriately).

North Anna River: Battle fought over the river crossing of the North Anna River in May 1864 as part of Ulysses Grant's Overland Campaign against Richmond.

Northwest Ordinance (1787): Organizing measure adopted under the Articles of Confederation that disallowed slavery in the Northwest Territory (Ohio, Indiana, Michigan, Illinois, Wisconsin) during its territorial phase.

Political economy: The study of how political forms are shaped by economic theory and practice.

Popular sovereignty: Political doctrine first argued by Lewis Cass but identified with Stephen A. Douglas as a solution for the political turmoil in Congress over slavery by allowing residents of the territories to decide for themselves whether or not to legalize slavery.

Prize Cases **(1863)**: A combined suit brought by the owners of ships seized by the U.S. Navy's blockade of the South and used by Chief Justice Taney as a test case for Lincoln's presidential war-making powers. The legality of the blockade was upheld by a vote of five to four.

Republicans: A "fusion" party begun in 1854 and joined by Lincoln in 1856, combining Northern Whigs and Northern Democrats on a common platform of opposition to the expansion of slavery into the territories.

Richmond: Capital of the commonwealth of Virginia and capital of the Confederate States of America (1861–1865).

Secession: The doctrine that the federal Union, being composed of sovereign states, could be withdrawn from if any of those member states disagreed with federal policies.

Seven Days battles: A series of battles fought by the Army of the Potomac on the James River peninsula in June 1862 under George McClellan, which resulted in McClellan terminating his Peninsula Campaign and retreating to Harrison's Landing.

Shiloh: A near defeat for a Union army under Ulysses S. Grant in April 1862, which convinced Grant that the South would not allow itself to be defeated easily.

Slave Power: The belief that Southern political interests, relying on the additional political clout afforded the South through the Constitution's $3/5^{ths}$ clause, had acquired control of the federal government and were intent on spreading slavery to both the territories and the Northern free states.

Spotsylvania: Site of an undecided battle in May 1864, which was part of Ulysses S. Grant's Overland Campaign against Richmond.

Tariffs: Tax laid on imported goods as a way of giving competitive advantage to domestically produced goods.

Thirteenth Amendment: Constitutional amendment first proposed in Congress in 1863, extending the original ban on slavery in the Northwest Ordinance to all the states of the Union, thereby permanently abolishing slavery in the United States.

Veto ("I prevent" in Latin): Describes the power of the president to prevent congressional legislation from passing into law; a *pocket veto* permits the president to veto legislation at the end of a congressional session merely by refusing to sign it.

Vicksburg: Major Union victory in July 1863, won by Ulysses S. Grant and reopening the Mississippi River to Northern commerce.

Whig: Originally in English political history the "country" party, opposed to the "court" party and absolute monarchy, this became the name of a party described in 1834 by Henry Clay as the new opposition to "King" Andrew Jackson and the Democrats.

Wilmot Proviso: Devised by antislavery Pennsylvania Democratic representative David Wilmot in 1846 as a rider to an appropriations bill; forbade the introduction of slavery into any territories to be won from Mexico in the Mexican War.

Biographical Notes

John Wilkes Booth (1838–1865): American actor, son of Junius Brutus Booth and brother of Edwin Booth, also distinguished American actors. Southern sympathizer and white supremacist during the Civil War who assassinated Lincoln on April 14, 1865, at Ford's Theater. Pursued and shot to death, April 26, 1865, in Virginia.

Salmon Portland Chase (1808–1873): Lawyer and abolitionist who served as governor and attorney general of Ohio, U.S. senator from Ohio, and from 1861–1864, as Lincoln's secretary of the treasury. Appointed chief justice of the U.S. Supreme Court in 1864.

Henry Clay (1777–1852): Lawyer, U.S. representative and senator from Kentucky, founder and standard-bearer of the Whig Party in 1834. Described by Lincoln as his "beau ideal of a statesman."

Stephen Arnold Douglas (1813–1861): Democratic lawyer, judge, U.S. representative and senator from Kentucky. Challenged by Lincoln for the Illinois senate seat in 1858 and defeated by Lincoln in the presidential contest of 1860.

Ulysses Simpson Grant (1822–1885): Began Civil War as colonel of the Twenty-first Illinois; rose to brigadier general, then major general for his victories at Fort Donelson and Vicksburg. Appointed lieutenant general of the U.S. Army in March 1864 and forced surrender of Robert E. Lee and the main Confederate army on April 9, 1865. Elected 18th president of the United States in 1868.

John Milton Hay (1838–1905): Joined Lincoln's presidential staff in 1861 and formed a close bond with the president, as seen in his detailed diary of the Civil War years. Collaborated with John Nicolay in writing the 10-volume *Abraham Lincoln: A History* (1890) and served as ambassador to Great Britain and secretary of state under McKinley and Theodore Roosevelt.

William Henry Herndon (1818–1891): Lincoln's third law partner (1844–1865) and author (with Jesse Weik) of *Herndon's Lincoln: The True Story of a Great Life* (1889).

Andrew Jackson (1767–1845): Hero of the War of 1812 and seventh president of the United States. Carried forward the political philosophy of

Thomas Jefferson as head of the Democratic Party; opposed by the Whigs and by Lincoln.

Robert Edward Lee (1807–1870): American soldier and Confederate general. Surrendered to Ulysses Grant on April 9, 1865. After the war, became president of Washington College (later named Washington and Lee University).

Mary Todd Lincoln (1818–1882): Wife of Abraham Lincoln and mother of Robert, Edward, William, and Thomas ("Tad") Lincoln.

George Brinton McClellan (1826–1885): Major general of the Union army and commander of the Army of the Potomac (1861–1862); advocated a nonconfrontational strategy against the Confederates and was eventually dismissed by Lincoln in November 1862. Ran as Democratic candidate for president against Lincoln in 1864.

John George Nicolay (1832–1901): Chief of Lincoln's presidential staff and co-author with John Hay of *Abraham Lincoln: A History* (1890).

Ann Rutledge (1813–1835): Generally understood to be Lincoln's first romantic interest, she died prematurely of a fever. The nature of her relationship with Lincoln was sensationalized by Herndon, especially in *Herndon's Lincoln* (1889).

William Henry Seward (1801–1872): U.S. senator and governor of New York and influential Whig politician who turned Republican but was shunted aside from the Republican presidential nomination in 1860 by Lincoln. Served as Lincoln's secretary of state and narrowly avoided assassination in the same plot that cost Lincoln his life.

John Todd Stuart (1807–1885): Lincoln's first law partner. Elected to U.S. Congress as a Whig (1839–1842) and later as a Democrat during the Civil War.

Roger Brooke Taney (1777–1864): Appointed chief justice of the U.S. Supreme Court by Andrew Jackson. Wrote the decision in *Dred Scott v. Sanford* (1857) and attempted to restrict Lincoln's presidential war-making powers through *ex parte Merryman* (1861) and *Prize Cases* (1863).

Bibliography

Reference Works

Basler, Roy P., ed. *The Collected Works of Abraham Lincoln*. New Brunswick, NJ: Rutgers University Press, 1953. The standard collection of all of Lincoln's known writings, with annotations. Excludes Lincoln's legal papers and comments on documents made as president. Two supplemental volumes, with newly discovered Lincoln writings, were added in 1974 and 1990. Available in searchable electronic format at the Web site of the Abraham Lincoln Association.

Burlingame, Michael, ed. *An Oral History of Abraham Lincoln: John G. Nicolay's Interviews and Essays*. Carbondale, IL: Southern Illinois University Press, 1996. A collection of interviews conducted by John Nicolay in Washington and Springfield with prominent political figures who had been closely associated with Lincoln, including John Todd Stuart, Ozias Hatch, and Orville Hickman Browning.

Fehrenbacher, Don, and Virginia Fehrenbacher, eds. *Recollected Words of Abraham Lincoln*. Stanford: Stanford University Press, 1996. A record, organized alphabetically by reporting author, of Lincoln's oral comments. Brief explanatory introductions preface each comment, along with a graded evaluation (A through D) of the reliability of the report.

Hertz, Emmanuel, ed. *The Hidden Lincoln, from the Letters and Papers of William H. Herndon*. New York: Viking, 1938. Selected letters and short comments of William Herndon to a variety of correspondents (mostly Jesse Weik) on Lincoln and Herndon's memories of him.

McPherson, Edward, ed. *The Political History of the United States during the Great Rebellion*. Washington, DC: Philp & Solomons, 1864. An extremely valuable collection of key political documents from the Civil War-era Congresses (Thirty-seventh and Thirty-eighth), including the texts of important legislation, excerpts from speeches in Congress, and presidential documents. Successive editions appeared in 1865 and 1866.

Mearns, David C. *The Lincoln Papers*. Garden City, NY: Doubleday, 1948, 2 vols. Letters and papers by Lincoln and others from 1847 to 1861, from the Abraham Lincoln Papers at the Library of Congress, as donated by Robert Todd Lincoln in 1922 and sealed until 1947.

Miers, Earl S., ed. *Lincoln Day-by-Day: A Chronology, 1809–1865*. Washington, DC: Lincoln Sesquicentennial Commission, 1960. A comprehensive tracking of Lincoln's activities and movements, based on an exhaustive examination of newspapers, letters, and diaries. Available in a single-volume edition published by Morningside Bookshop in 1992.

Neely, Mark. *The Abraham Lincoln Encyclopedia*. New York: McGraw Hill, 1982. A comprehensive collection of articles on Lincolnian topics, including biographical articles on Lincoln friends and members of the Lincoln family, Lincoln collectors, and Lincoln issues.

Rice, Allan Thorndike, ed. *Reminiscences of Abraham Lincoln by Distinguished Men of His Time*. New York: North American Publishing Co., 1886. A collection of personal recollection articles, originally published in the *North American Review* (edited by Rice) by friends and associates of Lincoln, including Henry Ward Beecher, Frederick Douglass, and Walt Whitman.

Wilson, Douglas L., and Rodney O. Davis, eds. *Herndon's Informants: Letters, Interviews and Statements about Abraham Lincoln*. Chicago: University of Illinois Press, 1998. Transcripts of the interviews conducted by William Henry Herndon in 1866 with informants who knew Lincoln in his youth in Indiana, along with letters and interviews Herndon solicited from Lincoln's friends and political allies (Joseph Gillespie, Leonard Swett) in later years for his 1889 Lincoln biography.

Biographies

Arnold, Isaac Newton. *The Life of Abraham Lincoln*. 1884; Lincoln, NE: University of Nebraska Press, 1994. Arnold represented Chicago in Congress from 1860–1862 and was a loyal supporter of Lincoln there. He published a biography of Lincoln in 1866, but this work was based on a larger array of sources.

Carwardine, Richard. *Lincoln*. London: Longman/Pearson, 2003. Stresses the long-term continuities in Lincoln's thinking, especially his repugnance for slavery and his confidence in the openness of democratic society.

Donald, David H. *Lincoln*. New York: Simon and Schuster, 1995. The most comprehensive of the one-volume Lincoln biographies.

Herndon, William H., and Jesse Weik. *Herndon's Lincoln*. Chicago: Belford Clarke, 1889, 3 vols. Based on the informant testimony originally collected by Herndon and ghostwritten by Weik, this remains the richest mine of information on Lincoln's prepresidential years.

Thomas, Benjamin P. *Abraham Lincoln*. New York: Knopf, 1952. Still the finest single-volume biography of Lincoln. A balanced, well-written survey of Lincoln's life.

Indiana, New Salem, and Springfield

Angle, Paul M. *"Here I Have Lived": A History of Lincoln's Springfield, 1821–1875*. Springfield, IL: Abraham Lincoln Association, 1935. Narrates the development of Springfield from its founding in 1821 through the years when Lincoln became a resident, touching briefly on Springfield during the Civil War.

Simon, Paul. *Lincoln's Preparation for Greatness: The Illinois Legislative Years*. Norman, OK: University of Oklahoma Press, 1965. An Illinois politician himself, Simon describes Lincoln's four terms in the Illinois legislature with his own keen perception of the inner workings of state politics.

Tarbell, Ida. *In the Footsteps of the Lincolns*. New York: Harper's, 1924. Tarbell, also the author of a multivolume Lincoln biography, traces the ancestry of Lincoln from the 17th-century Lincolns of Massachusetts to the 18th-century Kentucky Lincolns.

Thomas, Benjamin P. *Lincoln's New Salem*. Springfield, IL: Abraham Lincoln Association, 1934. A brief and entertaining description of life in New Salem, Illinois, at the time of Lincoln's residence there.

Walsh, John Evangelist. *The Shadows Rise: Abraham Lincoln and the Ann Rutledge Legend*. Urbana, IL: University of Illinois Press, 1993. A strong advocate of the reliability of accounts of Lincoln's New Salem years, which linked him romantically with Ann Rutledge.

Warren, Louis. *Lincoln's Youth: Indiana Years, 1816–1830*. Indianapolis: Indiana Historical Society, 1959. An exceptionally detailed history of Lincoln's growth and maturation from 1816 to 1830, with attention to his schooling, family, and first jobs.

Wilson, Douglas L. *Honor's Voice: The Transformation of Abraham Lincoln*. New York: Knopf, 1998. Focuses on several key incidents in Lincoln's young adulthood, indicating how central the concept of honor became for Lincoln.

———. *Lincoln before Washington: New Perspectives on the Illinois Years*. Urbana, IL: University of Illinois Press, 1997. Key essays on the reliability of the Ann Rutledge story, on Lincoln's courtship of Mary Todd, on Lincoln's abortive duel with James Shields, and other topics.

Winkle, Kenneth. *The Young Eagle: The Rise of Abraham Lincoln.* Dallas: Taylor, 2001. A social history of Lincoln's young adult years, placing him against the social profiles of contemporaneous Springfielders and concluding that Lincoln was, in many ways, typical of the young professional men of his generation.

Lincoln as a Lawyer

Boritt, Gabor S. *Lincoln and the Economics of the American Dream.* Memphis: Memphis State University Press, 1978. Stresses Lincoln's consistent support for economic open-endedness and mobility within a market economy and tracks Whig economic views that governed his thinking as president. A highly influential study.

Davis, Cullom, et al. *The Law Practice of Abraham Lincoln: Complete Documentary Edition.* Chicago: University of Illinois Press, 2000. An exhaustive database of the Lincoln legal practice, comprising more than 100,000 documents from the 5,000 cases Lincoln and his partners handled from 1837 until Lincoln's death.

Frank, John P. *Lincoln as a Lawyer.* Chicago: University of Illinois Press, 1961. A brief survey of Lincoln's legal practice, embracing the nature of the practice, Lincoln's legal thinking, and the ways in which his profession affected his decisions as president.

Fraysse, Olivier. *Lincoln, Land and Labor, 1809–1860.* Urbana, IL: University of Illinois Press, 1988. A strongly argued analysis of how Lincoln's experience of Indian relations, land law, and free labor shaped his ideological loyalties and made him an ally of railroad capitalism in Illinois.

Pratt, Harry E. *The Personal Finances of Abraham Lincoln.* Springfield, IL: Abraham Lincoln Association, 1943. A careful accounting of Lincoln's property-owning and increasing wealth from his law practice. Effectively disposes of the myth that Lincoln was uninterested in achieving prosperity and success from law.

Walsh, John Evangelist. *Moonlight: Abraham Lincoln and the Almanac Trial.* New York: St. Martin's, 2000. A detailed examination of Lincoln's most famous trial, defending Duff Armstrong (the son of his New Salem friend Jack Armstrong) on a murder charge in 1858.

Lincoln's Political Emergence

Fehrenbacher, Don E. *Prelude to Greatness: Lincoln in the 1850's.* Stanford: Stanford University Press, 1964. A series of loosely jointed but perceptive chapters on Lincoln's return to political life after 1854, with particular focus on the 1858 senatorial race against Stephen A. Douglas.

Holt, Michael F. *The Rise and Fall of the American Whig Party: Jacksonian Politics and the Onset of the Civil War.* New York: Oxford University Press, 1999. An enormous, highly detailed history of the fortunes of the Whig Party, with particular attention to its organization for elections and its successes and failures on the state and local levels, including Lincoln and Illinois.

Holzer, Harold. *Lincoln at Cooper Union: The Speech That Made Abraham Lincoln President.* New York: Simon & Schuster, 2004. A brief but engagingly written book about the creation and delivery of the Cooper Institute speech of February 27, 1860.

Howe, Daniel Walker. *The Political Culture of the American Whigs.* Chicago: University of Chicago Press, 1979. Classic explanation of the values and attitudes that stood behind the public policies of the Whigs, with separate chapters on the major Whig leaders, including a chapter on Lincoln that is one of the best essays ever written about Lincoln and the ideas of the Whig party.

Jaffa, Harry V. *Crisis of the House Divided: An Interpretation of the Issues in the Lincoln-Douglas Debates.* Garden City, NY: Doubleday, 1959. A brilliant and painstaking analysis of the issues at stake in the Lincoln-Douglas debates and the way in which Lincoln and Douglas debated these issues in the 1858 Illinois senatorial race. Makes a powerful argument for the centrality of moral considerations in Lincoln's opposition to Douglas, while condemning Douglas's amoral politics. Probably the finest Lincoln book written in the 20th century.

Riddle, Donald. *Lincoln Runs for Congress.* New Brunswick, NJ: Rutgers University Press, 1948. A brief narrative of Lincoln's bid for a seat in the House of Representatives in 1847, with an analysis of Lincoln's district and the difficult path he had to negotiate to obtain the Whig nomination for the seat.

Sigelshiffer, Saul. *The American Conscience: The Drama of the Lincoln-Douglas Debates.* New York: Horizon, 1975. A lengthy account, debate by debate, of the "joint discussions" held between Lincoln and Douglas in

1858 as Lincoln struggled to remove Douglas from his seat in the U.S. Senate.

Sparks, E. Earle, ed. *The Lincoln-Douglas Debates of 1858: Collections of the Illinois State Historical Library*, vol. 3. Springfield, IL: Illinois State Historical Library, 1908. The most important edition of the texts of the Lincoln-Douglas debates, containing (in addition to the debates) the texts of newspaper accounts of the seven debates. The text of the debates is also contained in *The Collected Works* (Basler edition).

Lincoln's Presidency

Burlingame, Michael, and J. T. Ettlinger, eds. *Inside Lincoln's White House: The Complete Civil War Diary of John Hay.* Carbondale, IL: Southern Illinois University Press, 1997. The successor to Tyler Dennett's edition of John Hay's diary during the years Hay served as part of Lincoln's White House staff. Ettlinger prepared the original text; Burlingame completed the project and added substantial explanatory footnotes.

Carpenter, Francis B. *Six Months in the White House with Abraham Lincoln.* New York: Hurd & Houghton, 1867. Carpenter was hired in 1864 to paint an enormous celebratory picture of Lincoln reading the first draft of the Emancipation Proclamation to his cabinet and took up residence in the White House for six months. His gossipy memoir of those months contains numerous discussions with Lincoln on wartime issues.

Cox, Lawanda. *Lincoln and Black Freedom: A Study in Presidential Leadership.* Columbia, SC: University of South Carolina Press, 1981. A careful and sympathetic analysis of Lincoln's racial views, using his superintendence of the Louisiana reconstruction process as a test case of Lincoln's commitment to emancipation and black civil rights.

Donald, David, ed. *Inside Lincoln's Cabinet: The Civil War Diaries of Salmon P. Chase.* New York: Longmans, 1954. Chase was Lincoln's secretary of the treasury, and his wartime diaries are extremely useful for tracking Chase's attitude toward Lincoln and the work of a cabinet secretary. Contains a valuable firsthand description of Lincoln's introduction of the Emancipation Proclamation to the cabinet in July 1862.

Harris, William C. *Lincoln's Last Months.* Cambridge, MA: Harvard University Press, 2004. An evenhanded account of the months between Lincoln's reelection in November 1864 and his assassination in April 1865. Recounts six major problems Lincoln dealt with, beginning with reelection and including the restructuring of the cabinet and last-minute peace negotiations with the Confederacy.

————. *With Charity for All: Lincoln and the Restoration of the Union.* Lexington, KY: University Press of Kentucky, 1997. Surveys Lincoln's attempts to create Unionist regimes in the Southern states reconquered by federal forces; concludes that, at the end, Lincoln probably preferred to let the Unionist governments make their own decisions about how to incorporate the freed slaves into their new governments, without taking decisive federal action on behalf of black civil rights.

Hendrick, Burton J. *Lincoln's War Cabinet.* Boston: Little, Brown, 1946. A dramatic and colorful history of Lincoln's cabinet in its original configuration, from 1861 until the resignation of Salmon P. Chase in 1864. Marvelous character sketches of cabinet members.

Jaffa, Harry. *A New Birth of Freedom: Abraham Lincoln and the Coming of the Civil War.* Lanham, MD: Rowman & Littlefield, 2000. Focuses on Lincoln's First Inaugural Address and his message to the special session of Congress called for July 4, 1861; underscores the importance Lincoln attached to enforcing an orderly democratic process.

Leech, Margaret. *Reveille in Washington.* New York: Harper, 1941. A colorful, sometimes directionless, but always teeming-with-detail history of Washington during the war years and Lincoln's place in the life of the city.

Paludan, Phillip S. *The Presidency of Abraham Lincoln.* Lawrence, KS: University Press of Kansas, 1994. The best overall survey of Lincoln as a chief executive. Paludan stresses Lincoln's commitment to the "politico-constitutional" system, which promises equality but within the framework of the rule of law. Supersedes James Garfield Randall's multivolume *Lincoln the President* (1945–1955).

Pinsker, Matthew. *Lincoln's Sanctuary: Abraham Lincoln and the Soldiers' Home.* New York: Oxford University Press, 2003. The first account of Lincoln and the Soldiers' Home, the summer White House that Lincoln used in the summers of 1862, 1863, and 1864.

Potter, David. *Lincoln and His Party in the Secession Crisis.* Baton Rouge, LA: Louisiana State University Press, 1995. Originally published in 1942, this is the classic account of Lincoln's failed attempt to avoid the outbreak of civil war during the months between his election in November 1860 and his inauguration in March 1861.

Lincoln and the Gettysburg Address

Klement, Frank L. *The Gettysburg Soldiers' Cemetery and Lincoln's Address*. Shippensburg, PA: White Mane, 1993. A series of essays, reprinted from the magazines Klement originally wrote them for, that deal with the various texts of the address in Lincoln's hand and the dedication ceremonies at Gettysburg in November 1863 for which the address was written.

Warren, Louis A. *Lincoln's Gettysburg Declaration: "A New Birth of Freedom."* Fort Wayne, IN: Lincoln National Life Foundation, 1964. A fully detailed account of the writing of the Gettysburg Address, Lincoln's trip to the Gettysburg cemetery dedication, the delivery of the address, and its reception by the public and the newspapers afterward.

Lincoln's Assassination and Death

Bishop, Jim. *The Day Lincoln Was Shot*. New York: Harper, 1955. A popular and lively account of the Lincoln assassination, without an attempt at sorting out conflicting versions of events or analyzing the motives of Booth and his conspirators.

Bryan, George. *The Great American Myth: The True Story of Lincoln's Murder*. 1940; Chicago: Americana House, 1995. The first great history of the assassination, noted for its debunking of various mythologies and its balanced account of Booth and the pursuit and death of the assassin.

Kunhardt, D. M., and P. B. Kunhardt. *Twenty Days: A Narrative in Text and Pictures of the Assassination of Abraham Lincoln and the Twenty Days and Nights that Followed—The Nation in Mourning, the Long Trip Home to Springfield*. New York: Harper & Row, 1965. Drawn from the Kunhardt family's collection of Lincoln photographs, this lavishly illustrated history of the Lincoln assassination tracks the progress of Lincoln's body from Washington to its final resting place in Springfield.

Lewis, Lloyd. *Myths after Lincoln*. New York: Blue Ribbon, 1929. A marvelously well-written account of the death of Lincoln and the various mythologies that swiftly grew up around him.

Steers, Edward. *Blood on the Moon: The Assassination of Abraham Lincoln*. Lexington, KY: University Press of Kentucky, 2001. A detailed examination of Booth's conspiracy, the assassination, and the trials that followed it, dealing with the principal questions of Booth's motivations, the guilt of those indicted for conspiracy, and the myth of Booth's "escape."

Lincoln's Ethics and Religion

Barton, William E. *The Soul of Abraham Lincoln.* New York: Doran, 1920. The best overall analysis of Lincoln's uneasy relationship with churches and Christian theology.

Howe, Daniel Walker. *Making the American Self: From Jonathan Edwards to Abraham Lincoln.* Cambridge, MA: Harvard University Press, 1997. Examines the creation of an American model personality, based on notions of self-control and self-transformation, which played significant roles in the formation of the Whig and Evangelical Protestant minds.

Miller, William Lee. *Lincoln's Virtues: An Ethical Biography.* New York: Knopf, 2002. An engagingly well-written survey of Lincoln's connection of morality with public policy, from his youth to the election of 1860.

Lincoln in Photographs

Hamilton, Charles, and Lloyd Ostendorf. *Lincoln in Photographs: An Album of Every Known Pose.* Norman, OK: University of Oklahoma Press, 1963. An exhaustive catalogue of every authentic photograph taken of Lincoln, with information on the photographers and circumstances surrounding each photograph.

Holzer, Harold, Mark Neely, and Gabor S. Boritt. *The Lincoln Image: Abraham Lincoln and the Popular Print.* New York: Scribner's, 1984. Originally an exhibition of popular Lincoln prints of the 1860s, this volume illustrates the ways in which Americans and the American print-making industry attempted to visualize Lincoln when he burst into national prominence as the Republican presidential nominee in 1860.

Kunhardt, Philip, et al. *Lincoln: An Illustrated Biography.* New York: Knopf, 1992. Created as a companion to the 1992 PBS series *Lincoln*, this gorgeously laid-out book teems with period photographs, sidebars, and an excellent narrative of Lincoln's life.

Lorant, Stefan. *Lincoln: A Picture Story of His Life.* New York: Harper & Brothers, 1952. A photographic biography. Lorant's text briefly sketches the outlines of Lincoln's life and copiously illustrates it with photographs, prints, and documents of Lincoln and his contemporaries.

Mellon, James, ed. *The Face of Lincoln.* New York: Viking, 1979. A beautifully crafted oversize volume of Lincoln photographs, with excerpts from contemporary accounts of Lincoln.

Mary Todd Lincoln

Baker, Jean H. *Mary Todd Lincoln: A Biography*. New York: Norton, 1987. The standard biography of Mary Todd Lincoln, defending her from her detractors and urging a new understanding of Mary Lincoln as a political partner with her husband.

Essays on Lincoln

Boritt, Gabor S., ed. *The Lincoln Enigma: The Changing Faces of an American Icon*. New York: Oxford University Press, 2001. Eight essays on various aspects of Lincoln's public and private worlds, including Jean Baker on the Lincoln marriage, Douglas Wilson on the young Lincoln, and David Donald on Lincoln as a war president.

Burlingame, Michael. *The Inner World of Abraham Lincoln*. Urbana, IL: University of Illinois Press, 1994. Based on an extraordinary array of documentary resources, Burlingame assembles nine essays on Lincoln's character at midlife, touching on Lincoln's anger, his unhappy relationship with his father, his habit of developing surrogate-son relationships, and the unhappiness of the Lincoln marriage. One of the great Lincoln books of the last 20 years.

Fehrenbacher, Don E. *Lincoln in Text and Context*. Stanford: Stanford University Press, 1987. Nineteen short essays by a master Lincoln interpreter, ranging from Lincoln's relationship with his Illinois political rivals to Lincoln in fiction.

Lincoln's Legacy

Farber, Daniel. *Lincoln's Constitution*. Chicago: University of Chicago Press, 2003. Examines Lincoln's record as a defender of the Constitution under the pressure of civil war, analyzing Lincoln's treatment of civil rights, presidential war powers, the permanence of the Union, and the survival of the rule of law.

Peterson, Merrill D. *Lincoln in American Memory*. New York: Oxford University Press, 1994. The premier survey of the various ways Lincoln has been incorporated and reshaped in American culture, such as Savior of the Union, Great Emancipator, Man of the People, First American, and the Self-Made Man.

Schwartz, Barry. *Abraham Lincoln and the Forge of National Memory*. Chicago: University of Chicago Press, 2000. A controversial and vigorous examination of the ways in which the memory of Lincoln was contested in the generation after his death, then transformed so that Lincoln could emerge in the Progressive Era as the model American and the "people's president."

Internet Sources

Abraham Lincoln Association (ALA): The principal national organization dedicated to the study of Abraham Lincoln, headquartered in Springfield, Illinois. The ALA Web site allows visitors to conduct searches of digitized text of *The Complete Works of Abraham Lincoln* (Basler edition). http://www.alincolnassoc.com/.

Abraham Lincoln On-Line: An online resource offering news of Lincoln studies, links to Lincoln-related history sites, and reviews of Lincoln books. http://showcase.netins.net/web/creative/lincoln.html.

Mr. Lincoln's Virtual Library: A project of the Library of Congress and the Lincoln Studies Center at Knox College that features digitized and transcribed materials from Lincoln's presidential papers and correspondence, as well as other Lincoln materials from the collections of the Library of Congress. http://memory.loc.gov/ammem/alhtml/alhome.html.

Mr. Lincoln's White House: A project of the Gilder-Lehrman Institute, with coverage and resources on every aspect of the Lincoln presidency. http://www.mrlincolnswhitehouse.org/.

The Papers of Abraham Lincoln: A new project of the Illinois Historical and Preservation Agency to create a comprehensive successor edition to the Basler edition of *The Complete Works of Abraham Lincoln.* http://www.papersofabrahamlincoln.org.

Notes

Notes

Notes